hajc

123

JUL 2023

Baby Animals in the Wild!

Tiger Cubs in the Wild

by Marie Brandle

Bullfrog Books

Ideas for Parents and Teachers

Bullfrog Books let children practice reading informational text at the earliest reading levels. Repetition, familiar words, and photo labels support early readers.

Before Reading

• Discuss the cover photo. What does it tell them?

• Look at the picture glossary together. Read and discuss the words.

Read the Book

• "Walk" through the book and look at the photos. Let the child ask questions. Point out the photo labels.

• Read the book to the child, or have him or her read independently.

After Reading

• Prompt the child to think more. Ask: Tiger cubs have stripes. Can you name any other animals that have stripes?

Bullfrog Books are published by Jump!
5357 Penn Avenue South
Minneapolis, MN 55419
www.jumplibrary.com

Library of Congress Cataloging-in-Publication Data

Names: Brandle, Marie, 1989– author.
Title: Tiger cubs in the wild / by Marie Brandle.
Description: Minneapolis, MN: Jump!, Inc., [2023]
Series: Baby animals in the wild! | Includes index.
Audience: Ages 5–8
Identifiers: LCCN 2022010143 (print)
LCCN 2022010144 (ebook)
ISBN 9798885240802 (hardcover)
ISBN 9798885240819 (paperback)
ISBN 9798885240826 (ebook)
Subjects: LCSH: Tiger—Infancy—Juvenile literature.
Classification: LCC QL737.C23 B72485 2023 (print)
LCC QL737.C23 (ebook)
DDC 599.756—dc23/eng/20220317
LC record available at https://lccn.loc.gov/2022010143
LC ebook record available at https://lccn.loc.gov/2022010144

Editor: Eliza Leahy
Designer: Molly Ballanger

Photo Credits: Mark Malkinson/Alamy, cover; Eric Isselee/Shutterstock, 1, 3, 22, 24; Juniors Bildarchiv/SuperStock, 4, 23tl; PhotoCrimea/Shutterstock, 5; Andrew Porter/Getty, 6–7; blickwinkel/Alamy, 8–9, 23tr; Gannet77/iStock, 10; Julian W/Shutterstock, 11; Girish Menon/Shutterstock, 12–13; Ronald Wittek/Getty, 14–15, 23bl; PhotocechCZ/Shutterstock, 16; Ingo Arndt/Minden Pictures/SuperStock, 17; Nature Picture Library/SuperStock, 18–19; powerofforever/iStock, 19, 23br; Marion Vollborn/ BIA/Minden Pictures/SuperStock, 20–21.

Printed in the United States of America at Corporate Graphics in North Mankato, Minnesota.

Table of Contents

Black Stripes

Tiger cubs are born!

They drink Mom's milk.

They grow.
They learn to walk!

stripe

Mom grooms them.
They have orange fur.
It has black stripes.

Mom hunts.

She brings the cubs meat.

They eat!

meat

Their stripes help them hide.
They learn how to hunt.

They practice.

How?

They play.

They pounce!

They climb.

claw

Their sharp claws help.

The rain forest is hot.
The cubs swim.
They cool off.

rain forest

19

They grow up.

They will live on their own.

Parts of a Tiger Cub

What are the parts of a tiger cub? Take a look!

ear

fur

nose

mouth

tail

leg

paw

claw

Picture Glossary

cubs
Young tigers.

grooms
Cleans.

pounce
To jump forward and grab
something suddenly.

rain forest
A thick, tropical forest where
a lot of rain falls.

Index

To Learn More

Finding more information is as easy as 1, 2, 3.

❶ Go to www.factsurfer.com

❷ Enter "tigercubs" into the search box.

❸ Choose your book to see a list of websites.